m o v i n g l i n e
moving line moving line
moving line

moving line

moving line moving line

moving line

DRAWINGS BY CHANNING PENNA

First published in 2008 by
BOSTON PUBLIC LIBRARY
700 Boylston Street
Boston, Massachusetts 02116

ISBN 0-89073-133-0

For information contact:
Channing Penna
Post Office Box 610008
Newton, Massachusetts 02461
www.channingpenna.com

FIRST EDITION
Printed in Canada

Interior design by Daniel E. Pritchard

m o v i n g l i n e

moving line moving line moving line

moving line

for Tony

foreword

What is it that makes a person's adrenalin rush, pulse race, lip quiver? What triggers these primal, instinctive responses? Channing invites us on a journey to explore the exhilaration and terror of our very being. Her captivating pencil drawings, alive with motion and spirit, bring us to a place of raw, natural beauty – a place where the clutter and constraints of modern life are abandoned, where inhibitions are freed, where the untainted perspective of one's childhood is more than a memory. It is here, through untamed eyes, that we reclaim what is genuine and pure, where we discover, or at least query, that which first fueled the pounding rhythms in our chest.

Channing's portrayals of nature and people are startlingly alive, seemingly breathing before us. Flashes of vigor and energy are inescapable. The viewer is engulfed in a whirlwind of motion and, in response, is confronted with a deeper understanding, or perhaps questioning, of his own fundamental nature. Entering uncharted artistic territories, she captures the awakening that happens in the dawn of life, and how it reverberates throughout one's life, with the very tool that has been by her side all along – her beloved pencil. It is a thrilling ride. Take it. Or rather, let it take you.

by Brenda Kostyk

horse, eagle, wave

Come. Come close. Ride with me for a while. I cannot speak of the world but I can take you to a realm in which concepts rise out of mysterious depths, and visual sound gives voice to fleeting shadows, sudden understandings and curious calls for attention. Here is the burning point where I am alive and exposed, where primal signals beckon for attention.

After years of portraiture there came a time when I cleared the easel and began again, giving in to the desire to find what it was that made my heart quicken. As a child I had been captivated by the raging beauty of thundering surf, the rush from dreams of being able to fly, and the roll of drumming hoof beats, motifs that have intrigued humankind since the first person applied charcoal to the wall of a cave. Initially it was disquieting to discover that the flip side of this imagery would face me with my greatest fears. Amidst the majesty of the ocean lies the nightmare of undercurrent. A bird's wondrous flight becomes a need to rescue or escape. The electrifying cadence of a horse turns into terror of losing control. There have been many falls. Portraying what I fear has been as engrossing as what enchants, for both awaken inherent rhythms and offer a sense of the free and un-tamed. *movingline* tracks these sensations. While connecting me with a seemingly ancient inner tide, they are also an investment in surprise.

> *I know this, from actual experience, that an artist's work is nothing else but this long, slow journey via art's circuitous routes, to rediscover the two or three simple, great images to which his heart first opened.*

> ALBERT CAMUS (1913–1960)
> French writer and philosopher; Nobel Prize for Literature, 1957

sunrise

Unable to make the leap between the visions in my mind and the pencil in my hand, the paper before me remained blank. I was raring to portray the ocean in all of its fervor, but could not bring myself to form a single wave-like curve. Where had this impulse originated? My life had been lived inland. Swimming, aquatic sports and sailing held little appeal, and yet the sight and sound of moving water stirred me like no other.

So I went to the sea. The more I saw, the more I loved, the more I could not draw. I dove into the study of weather patterns, ocean currents, the nature of waves and the stunning statistics of water itself. Ninety-nine percent of the living space on our planet is under the ocean, which contains eighty percent of all life. Existence is comprised of it, regulated by it, contingent upon it. As Herman Melville wrote in the first chapter of *Moby Dick*, water *is the image of the ungraspable phantom of life; and this is the key to it all.*

Without waves my pencil finally touched the ocean with a drawing of rain at dawn. At any moment a rumble from above or a surge from below could transform the serenity into drama. It was a beginning.

> *. . . I heard a new voice speaking to me, not in any language I had ever learned but in the secret of my heart. It was the sea. Its come-hither murmur, its seductive roar. That was the music that could wash my soul. The lure of a different element, its promises of elsewhere. . . .*

SALMAN RUSHDIE (B. 1947)
British-Indian writer

massimo's shell

With all of my imagery, what thrills is the same as what intimidates: uninhibited movement. Attempting to portray a wave with a pencil was mystifying. I had once drawn a scallop shell and noticed that its contours resembled rolling waves. A closer study of shells revealed that while their camouflage emulated sand, stones, seaweed, algae and other creatures, their spiraling designs bore a marked resemblance to breaking waves, echoing rhythms, reasons and creativity that one could only begin to fathom. Shells were to become my blueprint for drawing the ocean.

Those waves! Soon I'm going to try once more to draw something wavelike. But how can you suggest movement on a static plane? And how can you simplify something as complicated as a wave in the open sea to something comprehensible?

M. C. ESCHER (1898-1972)
Dutch graphic artist

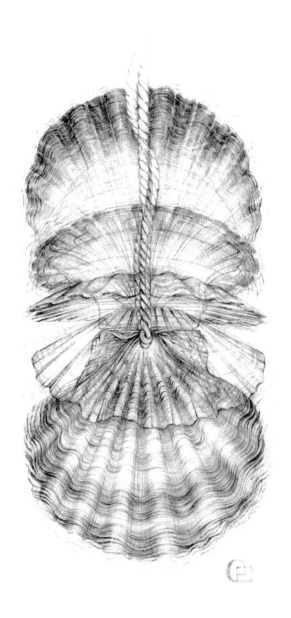

whirl

With drawing there is no standard, no method, no restriction - for art is relevant only to its maker and viewer. Its character and technique evolve out of deeply personal exploration. By nature, drawing requires sustained observation as well as interaction with the subject, whether animate, inanimate or imaginative. It is a different kind of education.

One of my medium's greatest learning tools is doodling, the more absent-minded the better. When indulged with regularity, it may be equated to a musician's scales, ever honing in on hand-eye coordination and the vital plays of the subconscious. Intimidation over drawing waves eased upon switching my doodles to shell-like forms.

> *I would like . . . students to pick up a pencil and draw a plant, a leaf, the spirit of a tree, the harmony of a seashell, formation of clouds, the complex play of waves spreading out on a beach, so as to discover different expressions of an inner force.*
>
> LE CORBUSIER (Charles-Edouard Jeanneret, 1887-1965)
> Swiss (naturalized French) architect

close up

At times, drawing is an attempt to infiltrate the inexplicable. How is it that a small shell can give a sense of largeness? We are told the universe continues forever, a concept nearly impossible to comprehend. Does this apply to the infinitesimal? Does the small spin smaller and smaller without end?

close up is what I saw in a shell that measured about an inch and a half in diameter. Viewers see it differently. I have been asked if it is my take on the universe, a hurricane, heat waves, maelstroms, a whirlpool, seaweed, tree rings, peaks and valleys, organs, hair, a centipede – interpretations which please me to no end.

> *When we try to pick out anything by itself,*
> *we find it hitched to everything else in the Universe.*
>
> JOHN MUIR (1838–1914)
> American conservationist

lone wave

The aesthetic pulse emanates out of a realm that may employ logic, but also defies it. To surrender to the wildness of the elements is to merge with an indefinable stream made irresistible by its potential for discovery and intimate embrace. Let it take me where it will.

> *There are unknown forces in nature; when we give ourselves*
> *wholly to her, without reserve, she lends them to us;*
> *she shows us these forms, which our watching eyes do not see,*
> *which our intelligence does not understand or suspect.*

AUGUSTE RODIN (1840–1917)
French sculptor

studies of a shell

*transitional interpretation
between a shell and a wave*

*although the imprint of the shell
is the foundation of this drawing,
it is only subliminally detectable.*

cascade

Beyond mimicking the classic curves of breakers, I wondered whether shells could instruct on other kinds of waves, such as the ones that eject straight up into the air out of clashing currents. Sometimes a piece draws itself, as though my hand is detached from my body. This is when time stands still. Here, what started as studies of a vertically positioned shell evolved into an intricate waterworld of falls, streams, ripples, sprays, swirls, tides, wind and sky, one line leading to the next.

> It is an intimately communicative affair between the painter and his painting, a conversation back and forth, the painting telling the painter even as it receives its shape and form.
>
> BEN SHAHN (1898–1969)
> American artist

spinning

Even though the life of a breaker is short, it has an eternal quality, perhaps because the next one is never far behind, or perhaps because it spins. A wave is a wave is a wave, and yet there is that light at the end of its tunnel. . .

It's a rhythmic universe we live in; everything alive spins and oscillates in rhythm. The sea, the heavens, the wind, and the stars dance their own rhythmic dance until eternity.

MICKEY HART (B. 1943)
American drummer

wave

When I was nine my grandmother called a family gathering to the Outer Banks of North Carolina, where eight foot waves offered rides that rivaled the board-walk's amusement park. My cousins and I could not get enough as we coasted up, way up and then down, down, down, up, down, up and down in a spellbinding flow that kept time with the roll of a distant drummer. One day the sea turned brown and the waves rose higher, inviting greater play. Innocent of the looming danger from an oncoming storm, a group of us ran in. Met by a deluge of rocks and sand, I found myself gasping for breath and struggling for shore when my fa-ther's strong arm lifted me to safety. In my sleep I replay the terror of that day.

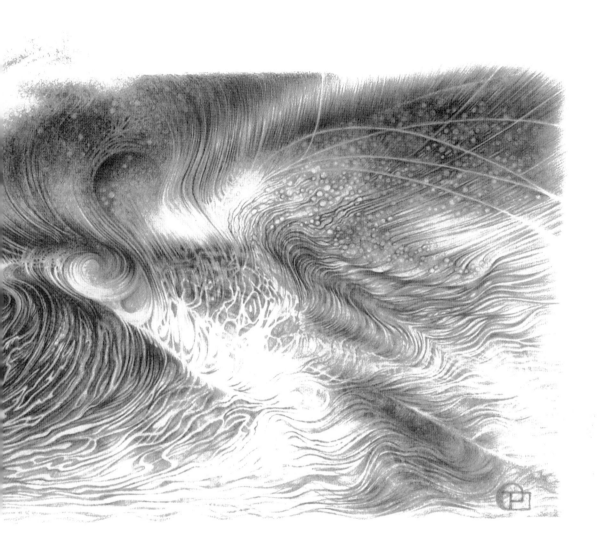

There are endless interpretations for dreams of being pulled out to sea. My own is that the ocean's grip is representative of human powers whose dominance is beyond reason and restraint.

I wanted to take what scared me out of me.

STEPHEN SPIELBERG (B. 1946)
American filmmaker

double wave

With portraits, I want to know people well enough to be able to mimic their body language and facial expressions, even to perceive what their reactions might be to any given situation. In drawing nature, while free from the critical eye of resemblance, the pursuit of character remains the same. Here I also aspire to identify with my subjects, which is sensational when it comes to the mercurial quality of waves.

Spend ten years observing bamboos, become a bamboo yourself, then forget everything and paint.

EUGEN HERRIGEL (1885–1955)
German philosopher

lightning

Like a snowflake, every wave is a unique representation of the whole, each a performance, no matter how small.

> *. . . the endless repetition of an ordinary miracle.*

ORHAN PAMUK (B. 1952)
Turkish author; Nobel Prize in Literature, 2006

breaker

On December 26th, 2004, a wave went from an object of beauty to a universal symbol of horror. For months, the heartbreak of the Tsunami continued to unfold. In its wake, 2005 set a record for the most named storms in a given year, including hurricanes Dennis, Katrina, Rita and Wilma. Their damage was catastrophic. Would people now turn away from drawings of waves? Was I to continue? There was no choice. Through all of the tragedy I was left with even greater awe over the life of the ocean and the ultimate reign of nature.

The day of the Tsunami, my husband Tony and I were on a flat and desolate beach bordered by dense brush, oceans away from the devastation. Had it happened where we were, there would have been nowhere to run, no trees to climb, no rooftops to clutch. I came home to draw a breaker many times larger than previous efforts. It is not necessarily a tsunami, for I do not know what one looks like, but a wave that threatens without mercy.

Chaos is the law of nature.
Order is the dream of man.

HENRY BROOKS ADAMS
(1838-1918)
American historian

jaws

The most daring of surfers are deposited way out in the ocean by jet skis in order to ride sixty, even eighty foot waves. We gape at their bravado as they emerge from such monumental beauty, awed by their defiance of danger. This wave is drawn at the three-quarters angle in which we watch them ride out of the tunnel. Although it is beyond my comprehension to tempt fate in such a manner, throughout the duration of this drawing I imagined the roar, the speed, the rush of adrenaline, the sensation of the being engulfed by water, and the relief upon reaching safety.

initiation

Artists and poets have been equating white stallions with the sea for at least as far back as ancient Mesopotamia (c.3100 − 428 BCE). While horses and waves are two of the three primal images in *movingline*, this drawing has little to do with their resemblance. Rather, it symbolizes transitioning from one realm into another. As a girl, I was taken by Douglas Lockwood's "I, The Aboriginal," in which adolescent boys in the Australian outback stepped into manhood through a hole in a consecrated rock after completing a long and arduous initiation. Open recognition of crossing a threshold strikes me as healthy not only for the individual, but also for the community.

> . . . *he allowed himself to be swayed by his conviction that human beings are not born once and for all on the day their mothers give birth to them, but that life obliges them over and over again to give birth to themselves.*

GABRIEL GARCIA MARQUEZ (B. 1927)
Columbian writer;
Nobel Prize in Literature, 1982

hoof

There have been moments when the research has been intense. At one point I talked my friend Wendy into letting me lean out of the window of her truck, camera in hand, as she sped alongside horses in race-training.

> *Once more upon the waters,*
> *yet once more!*
> *And the waves bound beneath me*
> *as a steed*
> *that knows his rider.*
>
> LORD BYRON (George Gordon Noel Byron, 1788-1824)
> Anglo-Scottish poet

shadow horses

There was a time on a large cattle property where, within minutes of mounting our horses, my brother Bill and I were racing at an all out gallop, side by side across an endless plain. A ranch hand caught up with us and warned that if we kept going we would become lost over the horizon. I looked out, way out, and all around. Everywhere the earth met the sky uninterrupted, not even by a tree. Caution entered in and we henceforth kept the others in sight, but that first charge of equine abandon has never left me.

Not I, not I, but the wind that blows through me!

D. H. LAWRENCE (1885–1930)
American writer

whistle

Afflicted with dementia, Dad could no longer speak, but he could still whistle. His caregiver, Charley, regularly took him to a farm where there was an old retired racehorse called Dimitri, who kept to himself. The attendants were continually stunned by Dimitri's ready response to Dad's whistle. Dad expressed his friendship with the old horse by brushing him with love.

reflected

To feel the motion, hear the hoof-beats, taste the dust. . .

When you change the way you look at things,
the things you look at change.

MAX PLANCK (1858–1947)
German physicist; Nobel Prize in Physics, 1918

cave horses

No art touches me more deeply than the spirited portrayal of movement by the first artists on record, more than 35,000 years ago. While the premise of *movingline* is the echoing effect of childhood imagery, its aesthetic quest is movement. Movement, movement, movement – because it breathes. Whether as energetically charged as a racing horse or as still as a shell, the portrayal of movement unleashes the viewer as well as the subject. In the late 1990's, I drew a portrait of a prisoner who had been incarcerated for eight years. She had taped copies of cave paintings to a wall in her cell. Their uninhibited motion gave her a sense of freedom

> *. . . as the interpreter of nature, one found one's self among cries and thrills which seemed to rise from the inner heart of the world.*

> ARTHUR C. BENSON (1862-1925)
> British writer

free fall

Go. Soar. Bring on your wildest self. Untame. Set free. Dance with the elements. Stare down restriction. Cross its lines. Allow for a feral sense of direction and your native instinct for play. No more curbing to convention. No more restraint. Go here. Go there. At last. Freely. Go.

Become one with the dusty world.

LAO TZU (6TH CENTURY BCE)
Chinese philosopher

response

My wish is for artists to be given space on the Op-Ed pages of newspapers. Non-verbal opinions can be of value. Here is my entry. One of them.

Before there was talk of war on Iraq, this was my response to 9/11. Terrorists. On our soil. En masse we turned. We warned. Little did we know what was to come.

On 9/11 Tony and I were trekking along a 1,200 year old pathway called El Camino de Santiago, which stretches across northern Spain. Out of touch with the news, we saw a replay of the towers falling when a village clerk waved us over to a tiny television behind her desk. With a son in lower Manhattan, a cold panic seeped into every cell of my being. Many hours later we learned he was safe. To alleviate my concerns and soaring protectiveness, throughout the two remaining weeks of walking this remote and sacred land I composed, in my mind's eye, an eagle turning to face those who would do us harm.

> *Nemo me impune lacesset.*
> *"No one will provoke me with impunity."*
>
> > Seal from an American Revolutionary War
> > Twenty dollar currency note (1778)

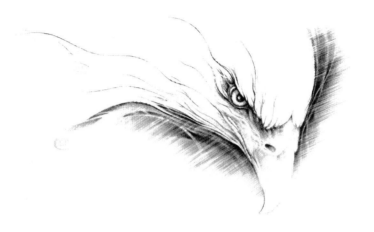

eagle

That eye. There is a commanding intensity in that eagle-eye that stares unflinch-ingly from banners, emblems, coins, diplomas. The eagle has eyesight that is four, six, maybe eight times sharper than our own. With the capacity to look forwards and sideways at the same time, it sees a rabbit from a mile away, or a fish several hundred feet below, and then dives up to 100 mph to catch it.

The earth is flat. I know.
I have seen its edge
with my own eyes. My toes
have curled around its rim
like an eagle's talons. In
the next life I will ask for wings
like hers.

MARIAN KAPLUN SHAPIRO (B. 1939)
American poet

mayhem

When I think "bird," the image that comes to mind is a dove. That it is a symbol of peace is a welcome coincidence.

In flying birds and earthly creatures,
in limber limbs of trees
and restlessness of human-kind
a liveliness of motion
is quick to animate
the living landscape of the mind.

ELINOR ROBERTS HARTT (B. 1918)
American artist

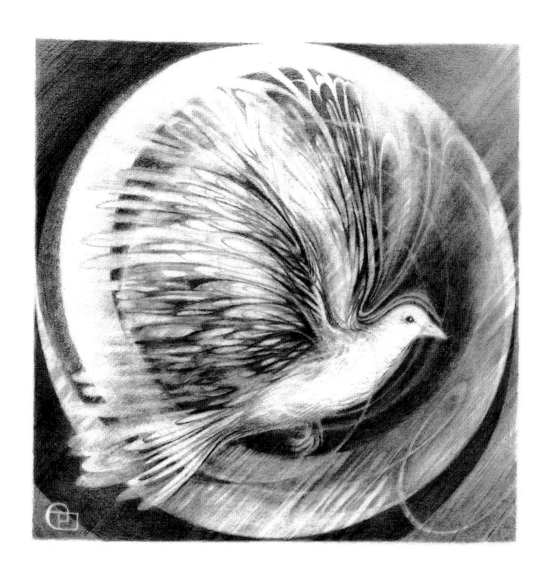

other side

In my experience, the wicked witch in *Snow White* is as monstrous as it gets. She ignited a lifelong fascination with the covert side of human nature. Part of the appeal of portraiture is the intimate process of coming to know the less obvious characteristics that make up an individual. Initially I drew this bird with a simple mirroring effect in mind. The result, however, is a projection into an alternate manner of its being.

Mirror mirror. . .

JACOB & WILHELM GRIMM
(Jacob 1785–1863, Wilhelm 1786–1859)
German writers

lasso

Once you have tasted flight, you will walk the earth with your eyes turned skywards.

LEONARDO DA VINCI (1452–1519)
Italian artist, inventor, scientist, engineer

mandala

tower

Tell me, where's the highest?

BILL T. JONES (B. 1952)
American choreographer and dancer

terns

I have watched terns holding steady over the ocean in gale force winds. Their flight is reminiscent of the gentle, poetic motion of butterflies, and yet they are referred to as the kamikazes of the bird world for their stoic tough-mindedness, their intrepid capacity to fish in the worst of weather, and their fearless defense of territory. Weighing between one-quarter of a pound and two pounds, they hold the record for migrating the greatest distances, some traveling more than 20,000 miles roundtrip between the polar ice caps.

If anything stops me mid-sentence, it's the sight of a hovering Little Tern above me. They look so beautiful, so delicate, but their conduct is anything but delicate. On the sandbanks they relate like touchy kids: "this is my spot, and you shouldn't step over this imaginary line, or I'll biff you!"

JILL DENING (B. 1948)
Australian conservationist

the call

As solitary as my life is at the easel, when I look at this title and ponder what my own call might be, it comes down to community – come unity. Perhaps one of the ultimate functions of the artist is to bring together people of diverse opinions into common focus.

Our appreciation of the crane grows with the slow unraveling of earth history. He is the symbol of our untamable past, of that incredible sweep of millennia which underlies and conditions the daily affairs of birds and men.

ALDO LEOPOLD (1887–1948)
American conservationist

CHANNING

And over the pond are sailing
Two swans all white as snow;
Sweet voices mysteriously wailing
Pierce through me as onward they go.

HEINRICH HEINE (1797–1856)
German poet

swans

At six I was taken to *Swan Lake* and was enthralled by dancers becoming swans. If there is a piece I have always wanted to draw, it is this first vision of swans dancing. Tchaikovsky's music can still move me to tears.

swan lake

two swans

The legend upon which *Swan Lake* is based originated in ancient Russian folk literature. It is of little wonder that Tchaikovsky chose it for his symphony, as the mating ritual of swans is a dance of swirling beauty. A sad historical footnote is that even though *Swan Lake* would become the cornerstone of ballet repertoire, its premier production in 1877 was a critical disaster and an embarrassment to Tchaikovsky, who never saw a successful production of his masterpiece.

Truly there would be reason to go mad were it not for music.

PETER ILYICH TCHAIKOVSKY (1840-1893)
Russian composer

migration

How do they communicate, taking off as a single body into the sky, and then switching directions all at once? Over miles of anonymous ocean, how do they find their way?

dance

In the realm of tempo, it is an easy leap between a bird in flight and human dance. For me, dance, from Fed Astaire to Bill T. Jones to *Swan Lake* to Flamenco, invokes energy and awe. The spotlighting of exuberance – that pinnacle moment of reach – is what I look for in every wave, bird, horse, face, musician and dancer.

In the very earliest times,
when both people and animals lived on earth,
a person could become an animal if he wanted to
and an animal could become a human being.
Sometimes they were people
and sometimes animals
and there was no difference.
All spoke the same language.

NALUNGIAQ (C. 1924)
Netsilik Eskimo poet

martha

Martha Mason is a choreographer and performer. As the Artistic Director of the Boston-based Snappy Dance Theater, she has headed this collaborative group whose style is both thought-provoking and irreverent. Touring nationally and internationally, they have delighted audiences with their theatrical innovation. Initially, I mapped Martha out in countless full-body poses, alone and with other members of her group, before realizing that the spirit of this portrait lay within the waves of feeling on her face as she is dancing.

mark and mercedes

Soft spoken and refined, Mark Sheldon's transformation on the dance floor was re-markable. Clearly the lead, he exuded self-assurance as his face evolved from the bliss of the waltz to the silent growl of the tango. Mercedes von Deck was weightless. Breathtaking in sequins and green-foam chiffon, she sailed through performances like a quetzal taking wing. United States and North American Senior Ballroom Champions, they came together as partners to create something flowing and beau-tiful. By day Mercedes is an orthopedic surgeon. Mark is a computer scientist.

carmen

Carmen Aguire, a native of Colombia, gloried in feline allure. In her world, song was an open expression of both body and soul. It was her escape, her credibility, her passion. It was life itself. The emotional range and breadth of her vocalizations could only come from one who had found a way of redirecting the effects of a difficult life into the release of song.

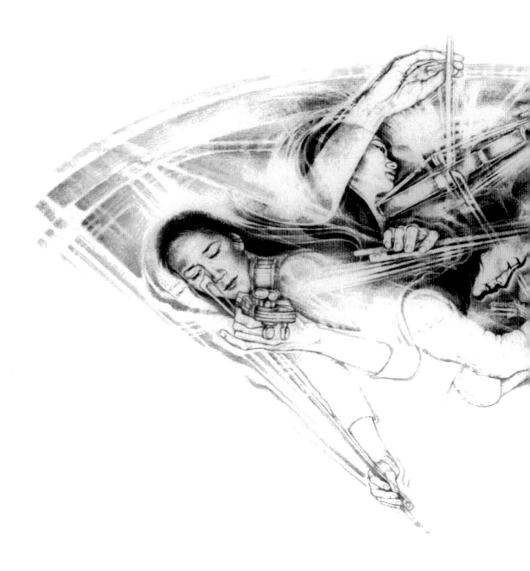

luci

There are a thousand beams of light whooshing around Lucia Lin as she plays her violin – a recognition that kept me intrigued throughout the long hours that her portrait was on the easel. Luci is a violinist with the Boston Symphony Orchestra and the Muir String Quartet.

seiji

For a millennial exhibit titled *Boston Faces*, I was granted permission to photograph Seiji Ozawa rehearsing with the Boston Symphony Orchestra at Tanglewood. Blissful as it was, all eight rolls of film were blurred beyond recognition. As I will not use anyone else's photographs for a portrait, this forced me to draw from impressions in my mind. He moves like quicksilver.

billy

On site for a portrait of Billy O'Neil, a giant electric crane operator, I was mesmerized by the guttural cadences of steel, stone, sand and gravel in motion. It is not a surprise to feel my beloved hoof beats, waves and wings in dance, music and sports. But in construction? Dozens of machines pulsated next to one another – one, two, three, left, right, up, down, everywhere. If not harmonious, it was unquestionably lyrical – an opus of vehicular activity, *The Dance of the Cranes*.

Everything in the universe has rhythm. Everything dances.

MAYA ANGELOU (B. 1928)

roger

What quickens my heart can be found in the most subtle of places and the gentlest of expressions. Many years ago I saw Roger Cicchese across a crowded room and was immediately taken by his quick wit and sharp intelligence, both easily detectable within the serenity of his face. Roger has been blind since birth. In order for him to experience the portrait, I described what I was drawing each step of the way. Readily following the process, he became involved to the point of giving input. It was Roger who suggested that I include his hands.

I shut my eyes in order to see.

PAUL GAUGUIN (1848–1903)
French artist

lauren

Despite the eight sequential renditions of Lauren Barnette's face, it is a still portrait. The movement is felt rather than seen. Knowing her since she was a young child, its flow has to do with the passage of time. Lauren is the Vice President of Operations at a Boston marketing firm.

> *There is a point where in the mystery of existence*
> *contradictions meet; where movement is not all*
> *movement and stillness is not all stillness; where*
> *the idea and the form, the within and the without,*
> *are united; where infinite becomes finite, yet not.*

> RABINDRANATH TAGORE (1861–1941)
> Indian writer; Nobel Prize for Literature, 1913

helen

This portrait of Helen Hayes was drawn for a New York City gala titled Waiting in the Wings, which celebrated the understudies in Broadway shows. The event coincided with her 90th birthday, and she was the guest of honor. I tell my subjects the more I understand them, the better the portrayal. Helen invited me to spend the day at her home in Nyack, New York, and could not have been more gracious. Here is where I rest my case that a still pose can be as dramatic as a crashing wave.

I cry out for order and find it only in art.

HELEN HAYES (1900-1993)
First lady of the American stage

dossy

The confluence of textures and colors in Dossy Peabody's home and dress are a visual representation of her imagination, originality and spirit. Seldom do I find a person's appearance an accurate guide to their nature. Dossy provided me with the unusual opportunity to use her self expression as the springboard for my portrayal of her. She is an Eliot Norton Award winning actress.

Life engenders life. Energy creates energy. It is by spending oneself that one becomes rich.

SARAH BERNHARDT (1844-1923)
American actress

robert

This portrait was drawn from watching a number of lectures by our then Poet Laureate, Robert Pinsky. He was keenly attuned to his audiences, hence the movement of his head, right to left. A comment he made concerning America's heterogeneity has been with me ever since: *Our impurity is part of our glory. Unlike homogeneous societies, we have no cultural elite. This is a good thing, especially for the artist.*

missy

On a hot summer's day after a Red Sox game, I made my way to the front of a packed subway car, hoping there would be more air around the driver's cubicle. As I edged my way forward, some kids were causing a ruckus. In no uncertain terms the driver told them to behave and they readily complied. I looked down to see that she would make an impressive subject. With minutes to go before I disembarked, I asked Missy Croke if I could draw her portrait. Here the movement of the train is expressed by the background.

kip

In a still portrait, movement is felt through a sense that the subject is breathing.
Months after drawing Kip Tiernan, the founder of Boston's Rosie's Place, Food
Bank, and Poor People's Fund, I joined her and a group of citizens at the Old West
Church in a five day fast to bring attention to, as she put it, *the legislated famine of
the innocent, adopted in the name of fiscal responsibility.*

aaron

Late one night my teenage son came home with a group I did not know. I could not take my eyes off of Aaron Firicano as he proudly owned his punk appearance and multiple piercings. As I dove for my camera, he readily assumed the persona of a defiant youth, taking pleasure in leering at the lens as though he were posing for an album cover.

bruce

Camera work is what I like the least about the process of portraiture. I take up to one hundred photographs of each subject, hoping half a dozen are good enough from which to draw. Hands down Bruce Marks, then the Artistic Director of the Boston Ballet, was the most at ease of anyone I had focused upon through a camera's lens. He posed above me, below me, and at every angle; he hugged walls, stood and sat on tables, dropped to the floor, peered around corners, draped himself over chairs, and dramatized with his hands – all without one moment of self consciousness.

CHANNING

anastasia

Hands are as expressive as a face, and equally as telling. By hiding half of Anastasia Lyman's face behind her hands, I made a play of opposites, for she is as approachable as anyone I have known. Her eyes are lively, focused and bright; her hands are of this earth. It follows that she is an avid gardener and cook, and one who acts on her convictions as a doula, and as a community activist against noise pollution.

michael

I look upon portraiture as biography, and do all I can to visually portray the breadth and depth of an individual. Here is an exception, for in the case of Michael Dukakis, the former Governor of Massachusetts, the portrayal is all about physicality. Having watched him for years in the media, I was amazed that in person his presence was so alive and dazzling. He is presently a Professor of Political Science at Northeastern University.

mel

On Sundays, Mel King and his wife Joyce Ida host brunches at their home that are renown for combining a diversity of people with great food. As a prominent educator, writer and activist, Mel's strength of character is a given. In coming to know him, what I did not expect were his stories of sitting on the kitchen counter as a child, or that he would be interested in my favorite garnish (nuts). His portrayal presented me with a line to be drawn, literally, between authority and tenderness.

I'm 75 years of age, and I've been an activist for 75 years. (April 2004)

MEL KING (B. 1928)
American educator and activist; Founder of the Rainbow Coalition, and the South End Technology Center at Tent City

al

Known as The Line King, Al Hirschfeld's humorous caricatures of Broadway stars were featured in the New York Times and other publications for more than seventy years. When I showed him the portrait, he looked at it with no detectable expression for what felt like an endless amount of time. Unable to contain my curiosity, I finally asked if he recognized himself. *Resemblance?* he replied, *Anyone can catch a resemblance. I am not looking for resemblance but rather at the drawing itself.* He then reached into his pocket and offered a caramel. Hopping down from his seat, Al took my arm and pointed to other renditions of himself that hung in his attic studio. I was surprised that he was short. Having interviewed and photographed him a few weeks earlier while he sat in his favorite dentist's chair behind the easel, he had given the impression of largeness.

> *Line as movement – prancing, skipping, twisting, and dancing – was the vehicle through which Hirschfeld conveyed the adrenaline rush of live theater and his absorption in the here and now, resulting in art that looks eternally, uncannily fresh.*
>
> MICHAEL KIMMELMAN (B. 1958)
> American art critic and writer

david

An artist can come to know virtually anyone by asking to do their portrait. That is what happened after hearing David Zucker give a talk on being a mime. Now a friend of many years, I continue to delight in the transformation that takes place when he takes to the stage. A man of multiple vocations (actor, director, author, poet and T'ai Chi teacher), David's mime is reminiscent of clouds morphing across the sky.

It is not uncommon to be asked when I will be ready for color. Does a violinist switch instruments after a certain level of accomplishment? On turning eleven, all of my gifts were art supplies. I wanted to begin right then and there. Although dazzled by the paints and pastels, it was the set of pencils that I picked up first and held onto evermore. Half a century later the basic pencil still feels new, like uncharted territory.

In early childhood, through experiences of wonder and exhilaration, there are conscious flashes of pure vibrancy. No future knowledge will inform us more completely about our potential. No attainment will be more empowering. No occasion will propel us more powerfully to a repeat performance.

. . . sharp nostalgia, infinite and terrible, for what I already possess.

JUAN RAMON JIMENEZ (1881–1958)
Spanish writer; Nobel Prize in Literature, 1956

acknowledgments

movingline has been a seven year solitary undertaking, supported by an extraordinary group of friends and one remarkable institution. In 2000 I was fortunate to have an exhibit, *Boston Faces*, at the Boston Public Library, and am grateful for the opportunity to exhibit there once again. Deep appreciation goes to encouragement by the former Boston Public Library President, Bernard A. Margolis, and to the assistance of its staff – Mary Bender, Deborah Exner and Emily Tenney.

This book would not have been possible without the help of David R. Godine, Sara Eisenman, Jennifer Delaney, and Dan Pritchard, and the generosity of Margo Winslow, Helen Rodman and Paulette Speight. A special thanks to my editorial team, headed by Trevor Thieme and including Judy O'Malley, Marian Kaplun Shapiro, Lana Epstein and Helen Rodman, as well as the commentary by Judith Wechsler, translation by Ellen Moloney Detwiller, counsel of Rob Rovenolt and Ami Bennitt, and assistance of Larry Goodier.

It would be impossible to express the importance of the support and input that I have received from friends and family, or to mention all who have contributed so considerately to this project. Ever at hand with clarity of thought, passion for innovation and keen advice has been Zeren Earls, who has nurtured *movingline* from its inception.

Brainstorming sessions with Chris Wiltz have been a continuous source of revelation, motivation and focus. Peggy Kociubes, never have I counted more on your viewpoint and responses. Dossy Peabody, what a comfort zone! Veronica Quarry, with every pun intended, I have drawn upon your wavelength and wisdom. Will and Anastasia Lyman, the birds we saw from your backyard in Boston, and the sanctuary you took me to in Louisiana, prompted drawings. The same is true of surveying terns with Jill Dening in Queensland, and horses in race training at Muskoka, the exquisite New South Wales property of Bob and Wendy La Pointe.

George Campbell, Mark Hopkins, Chris Roop and Tony Fiore, thank you for your technical guidance regarding printers, computers, scanners and cameras. Each of you has come to the rescue more than once. Others who have helped point the way include Maureen Alphonse Charles, Martha Mason, Sumru Erkut, Roger Cicchese, Shepley Metcalf, Peggy Sagan, Michael Simons, Jack and Barbara McCarthy, David Zucker, Elizabeth Bunker, and Carter Alsop.

To be a player in an artist's life is to show up in her work, whether literally or between the lines. My friends Roger Cicchese, Anastasia Lyman, Dossy Peabody,

David Zucker, Lauren Barnette and Martha Mason are here in portraits. Reverberating impressions of riding horses with my parents (Bill and Helen Rodman), brother and sister (Bill and Joni Rodman), and dearest friend from high school, Jan Whyte, are constant in my mind's eye – as is time, once upon a time, with Rachael and Conor Uris.

Simulating flight was central to my fantasy life as a child and remains pivotal to my art. When my sons Trevor and Brandon Thieme were children, I had the pleasure of replaying this pretense, and have tenderly thought about our times of "flying" together, and being together, throughout the days, weeks, months and years at the easel. Trevor, Brandon, you are my greatest inspirations.

There were a number of paths that I could have followed in 2001 after *Boston Faces*. At one critical decision making moment, Paulette Speight and Larry Goodier sat me down and said, simply, "go all out." Soon thereafter, my husband, Tony Penna, asked: "If you had no practical concerns, what would you draw?" In that moment, *movingline* was born. Tony has embodied the meaning of support throughout this journey as companion, provider, protector, advisor, editor, cook, playmate, and friend. Thank you, my love.

horse, eagle, wave Albert Camus, translated from the French by Ellen Moloney Detwiller, *L'envers et l'endroit* (Paris: Editions Gallimard, 1958) 31

sunrise Salman Rushdie, *The Ground Beneath Her Feet* (New York: Henry Holt and Company, 1999) 59

massimo's shell M. C. Escher, translated from Dutch by J. L. Locher, "Letter to his son George and daughter-in-law Corrie, 22 August 1959," *The Magic of M. C. Escher* (New York: Joost Elffers Books, 2000) 41

whirl Le Corbusier, *The Quotable Artist* by Peggy Hadden (New York: Allworth Press, 2002) 164

close up John Muir, *My First Summer in the Sierra* (Kila, MT: Kessinger Publishing, LLC, 2007) 157

cascade Ben Shahn, *The Quotable Artist* by Peggy Hadden (New York: Allworth Press, 2002) 80

spinning Mickey Hart, *Spirit Into Sound: The Magic of Music* (Grateful Dead Productions, 1999) 93

wave Stephen Spielberg, "Inside the Actors Studio," Season 5, Episode 504, March 14, 1999

double wave Eugen Herrigel, translated from the German by R. F. C. Hull, *Zen in the Art of Archery* (New York: Vintage Books, 1989) 77

lightning Orhan Pamuk, translated from the Turkish by Maureen Freely, *Snow* (Alfred A. Knopf, New York, 2004) 299

breaker Henry Brooks Adams, *Naturally Speaking* by C. C. Gaither (Oxford: Taylor and Francis, 2001) 100

initiation Gabriel Garcia Marquez, translated from Spanish by Edith Grossman, *Love in the Time of Cholera* (New York: Vintage Books, 1988) 165

shadow horses D. H. Lawrence, *Song of a Man Who Has Come Through, The Completed Poems of D. H. Lawrence, Volume 1* (New York: The Viking Press, 1964) 250

cave horses Arthur Benson, *Beside Still Waters* (New York & London: G. P. Putnam's Sons, 1907) 325

eagle Marian Kaplun Shapiro, *Flat Earth, Players in the Dream, Dreamers in the Play* (Austin: Plain View Press, 2006) 21

other side Jacob and Wilhelm Grimm, "Little Snow-White," paraphrased, *The Complete Grimm's Fairy Tales* (New York: Pantheon Books, 1972) 249

tower Bill T. Jones, "Keeping up with Bill T. Jones" (The Connection, WBUR, January 17, 2003)

the call Aldo Leopold, *A Sand County Almanac, Outdoor Essays and Reflection* (New York: Oxford University Press, 1949) 96

dance Nalungiaq, interviewed by Knut Rasmussen, translated from Danish by Edward Field, *Magic Words, News of the Universe: Poems of 21. Twofold Consciousness*, chosen and introduced by Robert Bly (San Francisco: Sierra Club Books 1980) 258

billy Maya Angelou, *Women Know Everything!* by Karen Weekes (Philadelphia: Quirk Books, 2007) 101

lauren Raabindranath Tagore, *Personality: lectures delivered in America* (London: Macmillan, 1931) 44

helen Helen Hayes, *On Reflection* (Philadelphia & New York: M. Evans and Company in Association with J. B. Lippincott Company, 1968) 233

dossy Sarah Bernhardt, *Madam Sarah* by Cornelia Otis Skinner (Houghton Mifflin Company, 1966) XVI

mel Mel King, Pell Mel, Tamara Wieder (*The Boston Phoenix* "Q&A," April 23-29, 2004)

al Michael Kimmelman, *His Hand Could Catch Your Essence in Flight* (Arts, New York Times, January 26, 2006)

channing Juan Ramon Jimenez, translated from Spanish by H. R. Hays, *Selected Writings of Juan Ramon Jimenez* (New York: Farrar, Straus and Cudahy, 1957) 98